After her graduation from The Walter Hoving Home, Leah attended Central Bible College in Springfield, Missouri.

She now lives in Kansas City, Missouri; is married to a Methodist minister; and has two lovely children.

This copy of LEAH is your memento of the Fifth Annual Fall Banquet—with the compliments of The Walter Hoving Home, Box 194, Garrison, New York 10524.

LEAH

LEAH

**Fleming H. Revell Company
Old Tappan, New Jersey**

Library of Congress Cataloging in Publication Data

Leah.
  Leah.

  Autobiographical.
  1. Drug abuse—Personal narratives.   2. Prostitutes
—Correspondence, reminiscences, etc.
HV5805.L4A3   248'.86   73-4042
ISBN: 0-8007-0595-5

Copyright © 1973 Fleming H. Revell Company
All rights reserved
Printed in the United States of America

LEAH

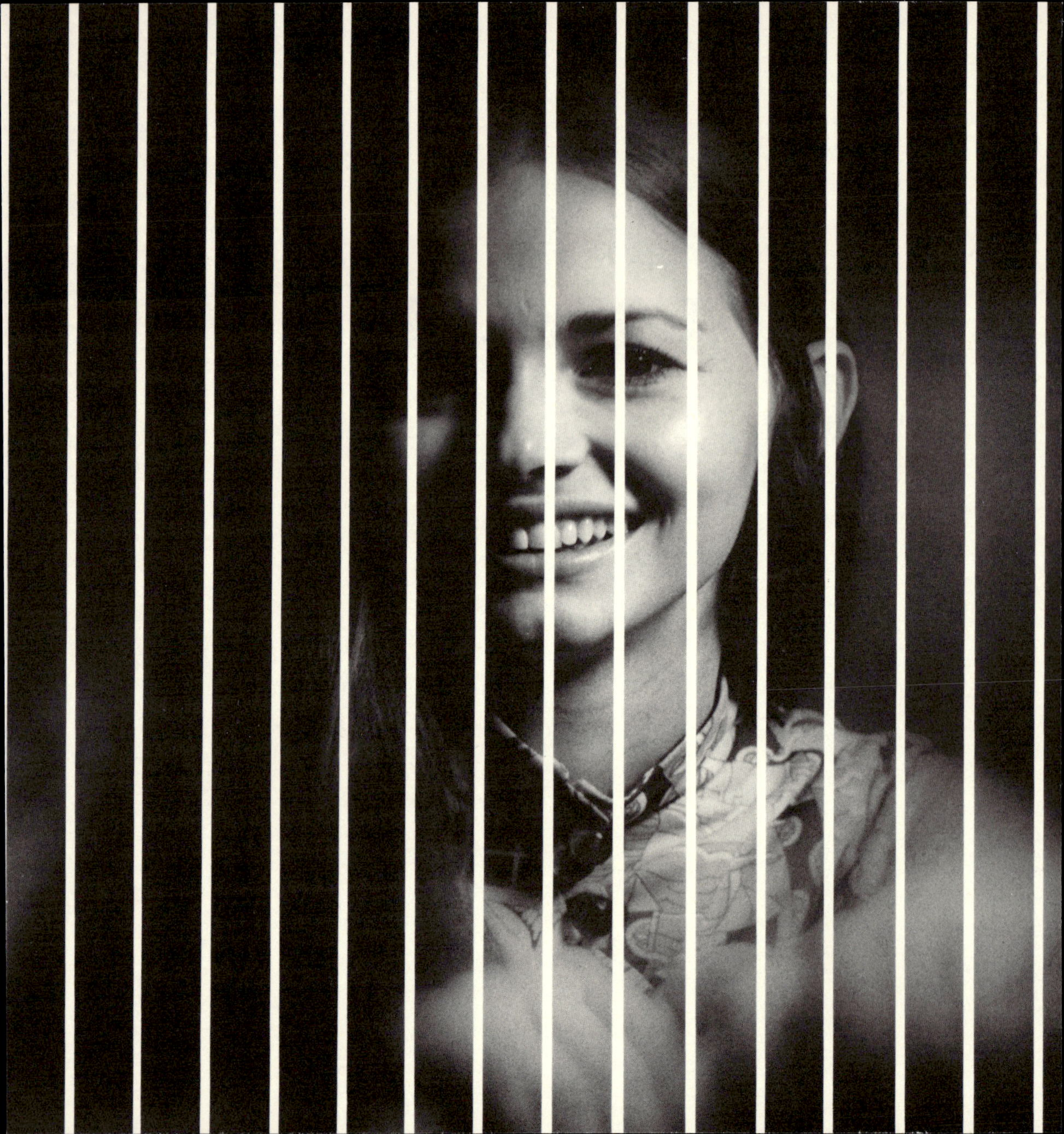

What's a nice girl like me doing in a place
like this?

It's hard to figure why I'm in this jail cell—not that I don't deserve it for the laws I have broken—but how come I got so mixed up?

A nice girl. . . . Take a suburban home, loving parents, good schools, and all the necessities of life, with a few trimmings, and you expect the daughter to be—a nice girl!

Well, I had all those things, but my cell mate put the story into words,

> You've come a long way baby—like down!

Yeah, I'm thinkin' about it. For four months I've
been scratching off days in this crummy cell and
today the judge will hand me three years. What a
bummer! Now I know how caged animals feel. If I
ever get out of here, I'm going on a campaign to
spring the locks in every zoo.

> By the time you get out, you'll be too old to care.

1

I'll still be a teen-ager.

> Yeah, a busted, broken-down teen-age parolee—
> that's what you'll be. But you'll be out—O U T.
> That's more than I'll be.

I'm sweatin'.

> Hot or cold, honey?

Cold.

> It's nerves. Too bad—sweatin' hot you could go
> to the infirmary.

I don't wanna go to the infirmary. I wanna go to court
and hear some square judge say,

Leah, you're a good kid, so blast on out of here.

> No chance. It would take a miracle.

I know. Instead, he'll bang the gavel and give me three years for peddling narcotics, practicing prostitution on the sacred streets of Houston, being a bad social risk and a hopeless drug addict.

Paying my four months debt to society seemed long enough. I longed for freedom and hoped the judge would be lenient. Underneath, I knew it would take a miracle and they didn't grow on trees.

I heard the matron shouting my name all the way from the elevator and leaped to the cell door in my cold sweat. The palms of my hands made the bars wet and slippery.

Court's in session just for you.

I had an answer but thought twice and kept my mouth shut. From every cell came some kind of comment:

Offer to sleep with the judge, Leah!
Cool it and watch 'em blow their lofty minds!
Good luck!

As I walked into the courtroom, my lawyer was talking to the judge and my probation officer. Their faces were frozen. I knew they were contemplating prison in order to keep me off the streets. After all, the judge had postponed my case five times, which is the maximum number of postponements allowed by Texas law.

I was scared!

My lawyer wanted me to look sweet and innocent and had asked specifically that I not smoke. He knew I smoked four packs a day. When I walked into the courtroom, the bailiff gave me a cigarette which I shouldn't have lit. I did and the lawyer was furious.

The courtroom was almost empty. I saw Mom but wasn't allowed to talk with her. The judge looked like he was biting nails and I knew right then it was too late for a miracle. He intended giving me three years. Sitting and waiting was hard. I wanted to hear my sentence and get it over.

While lawyers shook their heads and made notes, I glanced around the room. At least it was better than a cell. In the back row were a couple guys I hadn't seen before and figured they were reporters or tourists. My probation officer gave me a slight nod which I didn't understand.

The waiting dragged on so long that I became terrified. Finally, the judge called me up to the bench.

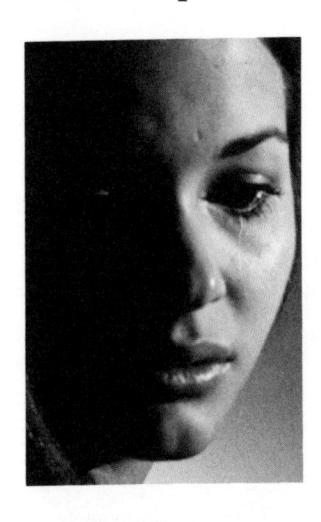

Young lady, all these people here are trying to help you and you just don't care, do you? You'd better straighten up, and you'd better straighten up good!

Well, I'm going to let you go with those people in the back of the courtroom. They are from Teen Challenge and they have more hope for you than I have. You will be on parole. You are to live with Mrs. Phillips for three months and not give her any trouble. I don't ever want to see you in here again.

Case dismissed!

He really laid it into me and most of it I didn't hear after ". . . I'm going to let you go. . . ." Teen Challenge people? That's those guys who were on the back row. I had heard of them because my cell mate loaned me a copy of *The Cross and the Switchblade*.

I couldn't believe it! I didn't thank him, or smile, or shout. I felt stoned on shock instead of drugs.

> I'm free!
> I'm free—
> not three years—
> no cells. . . .

I followed the matron out of court knowing I would meet my folks downstairs. Without conversation she opened door with jangling keys, then clanged the gates behind us. Her face looked like the walls—stone cold and dull grey. Every corridor was longer than the last and smelled of antiseptic used to cover all the other smells of a county jail. Without blinking an eye she unlocked my cell and shifted her head for me to enter:

> Pack up. I'll give you ten.

I'm free! I'm not going to the pen!

> They sprung her!

Amid shouts, warnings and sarcastic remarks, I grabbed my few belongings and waited the ten minutes for the matron to return.

What happened, Leah?

I'm out on a thousand-dollar bond. My folks are paying it now, then I'm to live for three months with a Mrs. Phillips from the Houston Teen Challenge program and be a good girl.

Teen Challenge? Isn't that the book I loaned you?

Yeah—and thanks!

I'm gonna miss you, Leah. Will you call my folks as soon as you get out? Here's my number. . . .

Yeah, I will.

Leah—all the way!

I ran from my cell, slowing only to say good-bye to a few jailhouse friends. Every time I stopped, old stoney face gave me the fisheye which meant—Hurry up! I've got more to do than get you out of here.

We walked back through the iron doors and smelly corridors, through the Booking Department, down in the elevator, and arrived at the bottom where a smiling woman and a young girl greeted me. The woman looked like a friendly enough native and the girl looked like an angel.

                I'm here to take you home with me.

I knew she was Mrs. Phillips. I must have smiled but can't remember anything except that I was getting out of jail after four months.

Mom and my stepdad were standing at the desk where a bully of a sergeant pawed through the purse he had taken from me four months previously. He counted out each item, checked it off on an endless report, and asked me to sign where he marked X.

It wasn't a particularly eventful departure for anyone but me. Mom had been through this six times before with me. She must have been wondering how long it would be before I broke probation, got high, ran away, got caught, and started the cycle again.

Without words the sergeant motioned me toward the door and for the first time in four months I felt wind whip my hair and squinted at sunlight without bars. The free world was beautiful.

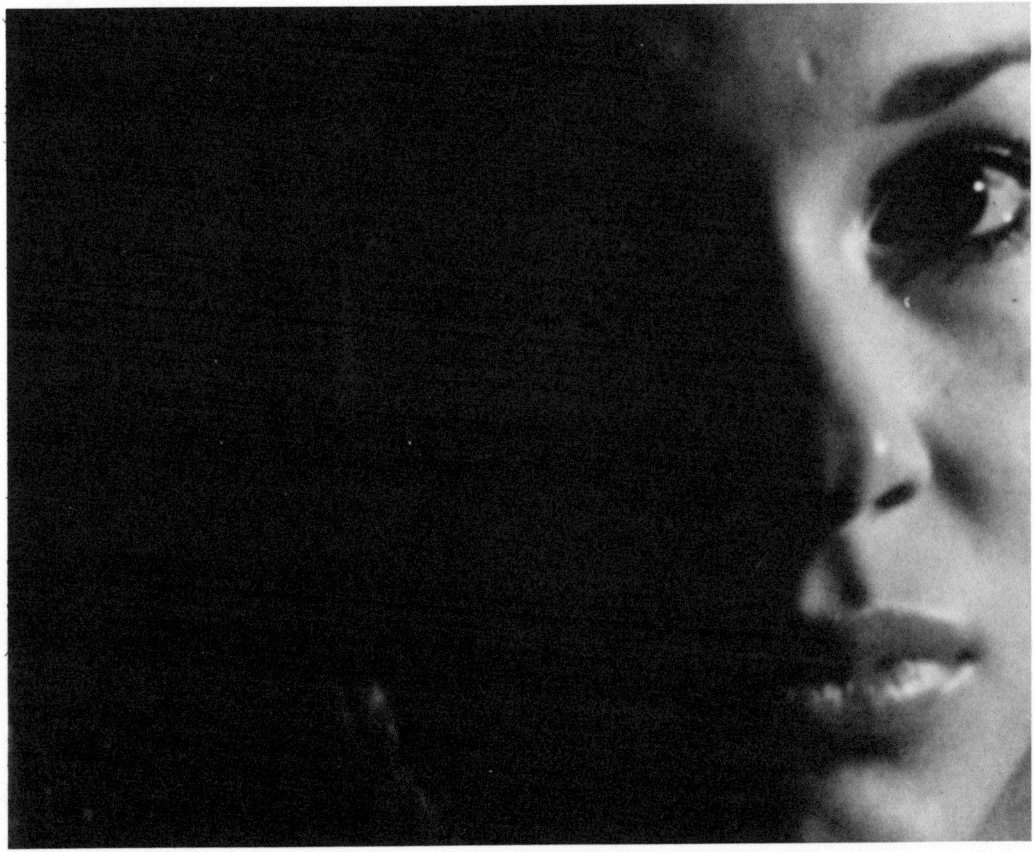

I didn't want to talk. I wanted to fly! I wanted to shout for joy and hug every free creature.

I opened the unlocked car door and did not lock it behind me. Never before had I noticed how beautiful the inside of a car was, nor how comfortable. Not even the steaming Texas heat slowed my exuberance.

I was ecstatic!

With new freedom I took out a pack of cigarettes and started to light up. Suddenly, I could tell that Mrs. Phillips didn't like it.

> Smoking isn't allowed in the Teen Challenge Program.

Some people! This experience is going to be its own kind of drag, but it's better than jail. Without comment, I tossed away what would be the last cigarette I have had in over two years.

Our trip to the Houston Teen Challenge Center seemed short because riding in a car again was something else.

> Hi, Leah. You're just in time for chapel.

Hey! You're the guy in the back of the courtroom.

> Right. I'm Don Ansohn. Welcome to Teen Challenge.

> How long you been on drugs?

About five years.

> Shoot heroin?

You name it—I shot it.

> Ready to change?

Sure.

We believe in the power of Jesus Christ to cure drug addicts. I used to be an addict, but the Lord delivered me. I've been clean three years.

I looked at the girl I'd been talking to because in the past five years I hadn't been clean three days, except during time in jail.

>Don't expect us to trust you, Leah, because you can't trust yourself yet.

Yeah.

We walked into a drab room which had chairs in rows and a table with a cross on it. Mom and Dad flanked me and we kept looking at each other. The singing was loud, off-key, and a freaky-looking guy in the back kept saying,

>Amen! Praise God!

I thought they were all off their rockers. When a fast song was played, everybody clapped to the beat, and during the sermon, my mind wandered outside to the sun and fresh air. The preacher was just loud enough to joggle me back with a few familiar Sunday-school phrases. I could tell Mom thought the same as I: Religious fanatics! What are you into now, Leah?

After the service, I was expected to go home with Mrs. Phillips to whom I was paroled. Sally, the angel, went with us. Mom understood and without ceremony I left, promising to call home once in awhile.

Could I get a cold drink? Haven't had one in four months.

As I drank, Sally talked to me about Jesus. I had heard of Him in Sunday school, but it must have been a different Jesus from the one Sally was talking about. Everytime she said, "Praise the Lord," I wanted to hit her. She rambled on about her new life in Jesus, while I thought about my own new life of freedom and wondered how long I could stay clean and out of jail.

At all costs, I had to avoid jail again!

Next time it would be the pen for sure. Almost as bad would be another harangue from the judge before he threw the book at me.

Mrs. Phillips had taken one other parolee and my probation officer said it had worked well. I hoped he wasn't putting me on and that he really thought I could make it with these fanatics.

As the evening wore on, three freaky dudes came in with Bibles and informed Mrs. Phillips that a guy named Lou was demon-possessed. They asked her to pray for him. She agreed readily and they brought Lou in. He wasn't a bad looker and I figured he had been hallucinating and probably was on acid.

Mrs. Phillips and several others laid their hands on his head and proceeded to pray at the top of their lungs.

These guys are a bunch of flipped-out acid heads, I concluded. They've got to be tripping! What kind of maniacs have I got myself mixed up with? I might have been better off taking the three years, because I can't imagine making it with these people. Questions came faster than answers, but I knew sooner or later I had to decide whether they were sincere, or sincerely crazy.

<blockquote>Are you saved?</blockquote>

Saved from what?

I wanted to get smart but held it, knowing Teen Challenge was not my second chance—it was my last chance!

Hey, I want to know what you get out of this Jesus business? Something must be wrong with me because I don't get *anything*—except mad!

<blockquote>Jesus is real, Leah, but if you want to feel Him, you have to open up and give Him a chance. If you don't try Him, you'll never know what you're missing.</blockquote>

The last I heard, He was hanging dead on a cross.

The last *I* heard He was alive and well and living in my heart. You know, one day I was praying and asking God to show Himself if He was real. Suddenly strange words started rolling out of my mouth. They were foreign words I hadn't heard before. It was spooky. Later I learned it was the baptism of the Holy Spirit which the Bible describes in the Book of Acts.

Yeah. I've heard about it, but I don't know if I want it.

More and more I was bugged by the fact that the judge freed me to be helped by these fanatics, but I wasn't sure of what they had, or if I wanted what they had.

For instance, the boy telling me about the baptism of the Holy Spirit had no reason to lie to me, and he wasn't smart enough to cook up a tale like that. There could be something to this Jesus of his.

As days went by I passed from fury and insensitivity to curiosity. The dilemma kept me thinking and plotting. At least, it didn't give me a cold sweat from nerves. I was calm, and best of all I was out of jail. Breaking away from Mrs. Phillips meant temporary freedom and then back to jail.

Going back to my old life would probably mean death, because many of my old acquaintances wanted to kill me for burning them for money and dope. I decided the old life couldn't offer me anything but a miserable existence and, ultimately, a lifetime in prison. This new opportunity offered me a resting place to get balanced again. Surely I could impress Mrs. Phillips for three months with good clean living.

What did I have to lose?

If this seemed like I was using them, I was.

Now, as I look back, it seems that the Lord had been trying to reach me for a long time. What about the time I went to score (buy dope) for Bob and overdosed while I was driving his car? By all odds, I should have been dead after passing out at the wheel and turning over in that ditch—or at least cut up from going through the windshield—but not a scratch! The car was all right and I didn't even hit anyone.

Then there was the time at Bruce's house when I crashed headlong into a bookcase from an overdose.

17

18

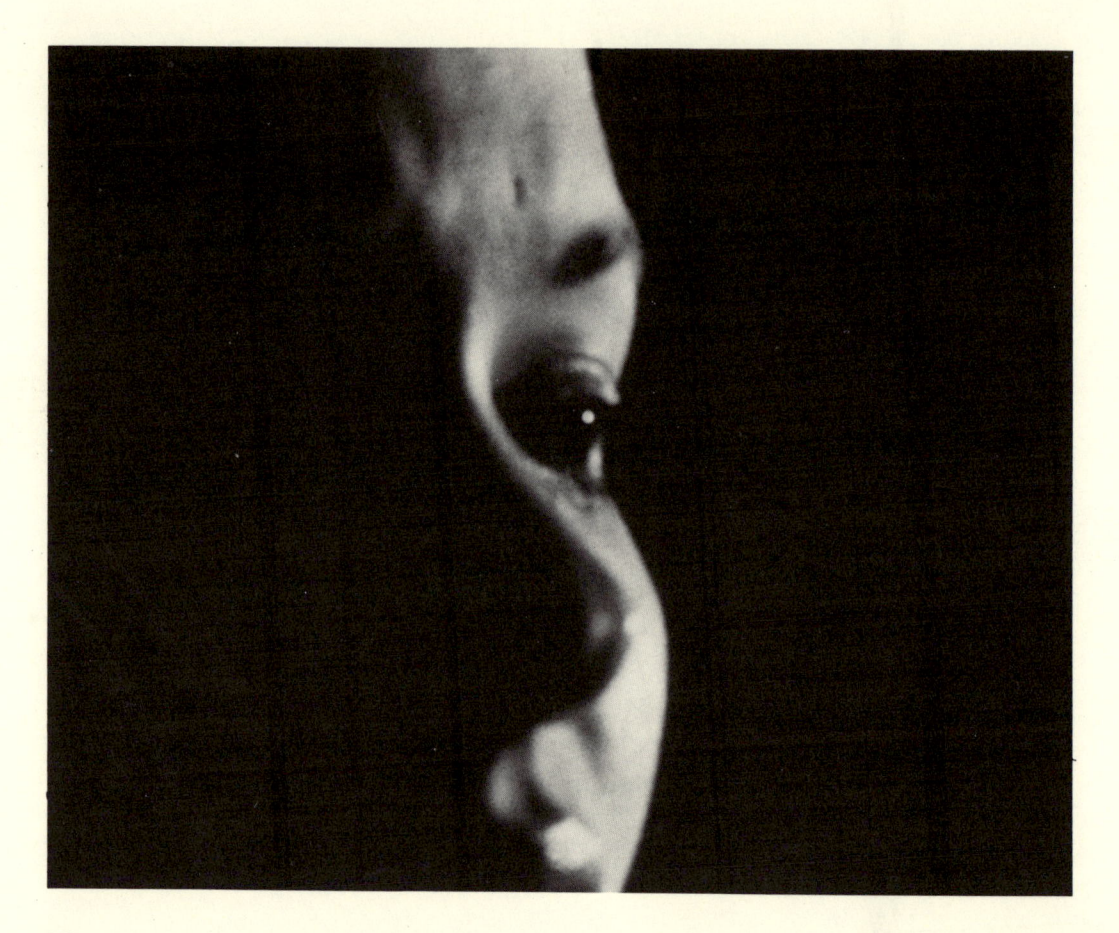

That time I was dead!

They couldn't even get a pulse and though I didn't want to live, I was afraid of dying. I couldn't do either completely.

As I think back, Lord, I never saw You or felt You. I never believed You existed, but I wasn't positive You didn't. All I knew was that if You were real and I died in my sleep I'd be in big trouble.

I'm sorry, Lord! *How many times have You heard me say it? Don't count.* You knew I wasn't really sorry. I was sorry only if I was going to jail, thought I was going to die, was afraid somebody would knock me off, or got too greedy on smack and accidently kill myself. You knew all the time that there was some hope for me, even when I didn't know it myself.

Honestly, I did not believe there was a way to get off my one-way street. I did not believe there was a way I could change, but I was willing to try.

For three months I lived with Mrs. Phillips, going to church twice on Sunday, once on Wednesday, and in between to the Teen Challenge coffeehouse where everybody talked about Jesus. Listening to them got on my nerves because I wasn't a Christian. They would come in, pray awhile, and run down the street shouting

Hallelujah!

What's wrong with them? I asked myself. They've got to be faking it. I kept watching.

Some of them told me they were high on Jesus, but I didn't believe them. I knew what getting high was and it sure couldn't be done on Jesus. I thought they were nuts. I heard them talk about divine healings and miracles. What if it's true, I kept asking myself. I mean I'd be stupid to throw that away. The more questions I asked the fewer smart-aleck answers I had. I began to listen more and flap less. Slowly I was opening to the Lord but only by telling myself,

After all, what do I have to lose?

For some time before going to jail this last time I realized that all my old friends were using me instead of me using them. Also, I was going to have to do something or wind up like all the other junkies I knew. But I kept on shooting dope and trying to forget. Then I went to jail again and began pushing the panic button when I was headed for that joint. I wanted to change but didn't know how, and here were a handful of people trying to show me and I was backing off. The dilemma didn't wear me down but rather made me inquisitive and thoughtful.

One night in church the preacher was going on about something I don't even remember and it seemed like he was preaching right to me. The guy with me leaned over and whispered,

>Where's Lou?

I don't know. Am I my brother's keeper?

>Yes, you are your brother's keeper!

I knew the preacher couldn't have heard me whispering and it could have been coincidence, but it just blew my mind. He took the words right out of my mouth. Was this the Lord reaching for me, or playing tricks?

I didn't accept Christ, although I made a half-hearted attempt to keep Sister Phillips off my back. She knew—but patiently spent hours with me poring over ideas and Bible passages. Once I got steamed up and threw a Bible at her in total exasperation.

During a church service, a crippled girl came in with one leg three or four inches shorter than the other. She hobbled up front and asked everybody to pray for her. No one but me seemed surprised at such a request. I never heard of such a ridiculous thing. They helped her kneel and slowly a few people gathered around and laid their hands on her. Prayers were numerous and loud but sincere and thoughtful.

> Let her walk, Father, let her walk. O God, let her walk straight and she'll give You all the praise.

Someone behind me was crying and I saw tears rolling down the face of the preacher.

They believed.

They actually believed God could cure this cripple. He did! I saw it. Her leg grew straight out.

It was beautiful!

One leg was a little skinnier than the other, but they were the same length, and I knew she couldn't have faked it. I was there, and she was not a fake.

It was a time of rejoicing and additional prayers. Everyone was moved to sing. I was so dumbfounded I couldn't say a word, but silently thought, Why would they fake it anyway? They weren't getting any money out of it or anything.

From then on it seemed like every service made me feel the preacher aimed his words right at me. Everything he said was like reading my mind.

Then one night as he was preaching I knew, *really knew*, that the sins of the world were mine. I have always thought they were the sins of other people. That night it dawned on me that Jesus suffered and died because of *my* sin. He died on the cross for me, His frail body exhausted from giving Himself to others. With overwhelming sadness I started to cry. All I could say was

Jesus, Jesus, Jesus.

Sobbing and crying, I completely broke before the Lord. It was beautiful! It was terrible! It was a personal miracle! *Lord, I can't go on the way I have been. I know You are there, so help me.*

I cried my whole self out and tears washed away my old nature, and the Lord came in. I've been a new person ever since.

Jesus set me free—
truly free.

Sister Phillips stood beside me and, when the tears stopped, I felt an inner peace that I had never known before nor since. From that moment I have been a new being, and when the Bible speaks of being crucified with Christ I understand.

Nevertheless it is not I who live but
Christ who liveth within me.

I understand that, also. Praise God! I am home free.

Oh, I've had trouble since. But, even when I have troubles, things aren't half as bad as before because I have Him to go to. I'm happy on the inside and have never lost the glowing inner peace that Jesus alone gives.

Now it seems that when I'm talking about my past life I am talking about another person. It doesn't seem like me.

He changed my life!

All the time I was on drugs I was looking for something. I was looking for an experience that was the ultimate experience. What could be more satisfying and more lasting than meeting the Lord? I knew that drugs from that time on had nothing more to offer me. I had been on an ego trip—an ego game that I was playing while trying to be somebody. Now I don't have to pretend at being somebody. I'm a child of the King.

Hallelujah! Hallelujah!

I remember the way I used to be—cursing, filthy trash, Lord. My old friends still think I am, but that's not really me. It never was me on the inside. It was an act I put on—a tough, hard image to convince them I was cool.

My taste in clothes, music, entertainment, friends has changed. I know everybody from my old life thinks I'm odd since I've met You. I don't want to condemn anyone or hurt my old friends, but I've got to find new ones. I'll pray for the old ones, turn them over to You, then close the chapter.

You know, Lord, my whole intention from the sixth grade on was to be bad. When Mom wouldn't let me join a social club, I set out to prove I had a power all my own. I was running with the bad kids. I was smoking and drinking and always getting sent to the principal's office. From then on, it was straight downhill.

When I was in ninth grade, I was drinking heavily and by the time I was in tenth, I was smoking marijuana. In my eleventh and twelfth grades, I was on LSD and speed. At seventeen, I was turned on to heroin and after that nothing else satisfied me. Heroin put me in a daze and the world went on without me.

It was great to avoid the world.

Getting high on speed and acid made me more aware of my inferiority complex and I was miserable.

The guy who turned me on to heroin was my boyfriend Randy. I dated him for several years, but my Mom didn't like him.

Now he is in the penitentiary for six years on a drugs charge. I pray for him but don't know if I want to see him again. Even if he was a Christian, I don't know whether we would have anything in common anymore.

Vividly I remember the night Randy turned me on to heroin. It was in a Houston apartment. There were six hippies living there and somebody had some heroin.

Wanta kick in five dollars for a fix, Leah?

Sure, I've never tried it.

During the next half hour, everybody went into the bathroom.

It's good stuff! Wow!

You can have it. I don't want any.

Come on. Why knock it before you've tried it?

Reluctantly, I followed him into the bathroom and he drew the stuff up in a syringe. My veins were so small he had a terrible time at first. Then he massaged my arms to pump up the veins and stuck in the needle. I didn't feel anything. We walked back to the living room and kids were lying around stoned. Suddenly I got a warm rush and slumped to the floor. There was such a weight on my head, I thought someone was pushing me on the floor. I didn't overdose, but Randy expected me to. I just sat. This new trip was different from anything before. From the beginning, I knew it was different —also from the beginning, I knew I liked it.

> You might get sick, so don't drink anything. You might throw up.

Someone suggested we take off in the car. I agreed but would have been perfectly content to sit and enjoy my new trip.

For the next two hours we drove around in a car and I didn't even get carsick. Everybody kept complimenting me and exclaiming on my tolerance level. I felt like a real hero being able to enjoy and tolerate heroin. After that, every time I got a chance to use heroin, I did.

My sis used heroin before I did, although she is a year younger. Her boyfriend was using it, too, but she saw him getting addicted and stopped short:

It's a one-way street.

I kept on doing it, and kept running with kids who did.

A junkie! Wow, that's terrible! An acid-head or speed-freak, that's okay—but a junkie is a dirty nasty.

Almost as if to prove something, I picked up with an older gang who were hard-core heroin addicts. At that point, I severed my relationship with the hippie world and chose gangsters. From then on, it was downhill—even faster.

Lord, how grateful I am that You took me out of the rat race. Praise Your name! My friends think I'm crazy. Well, I say let them think it. I know what I know: their coarse jesting and profanity seem senseless to me. I have nothing in common with them anymore. I don't even want to see them. I don't mean to turn them off, Lord, and I can't cram You down their throats, yet I feel frustrated not being able to tell them how great You are and how much I love You. Lord, show them what You've shown me, in Your own time. Lord, You know what it takes for each soul to see his own need for You. The world hasn't changed. I've changed. My old friends don't know what they are missing but don't let me get too anxious for their salvation, Lord. I know You're never too late.

Where do I belong?

When I was in church with Lou—he had been going to the coffeehouse and had become a Christian—kids kept talking about speaking in tongues as a badge of the Holy Spirit. I didn't know if I wanted it. It scared me, because I didn't understand what it was and branded it as emotional frenzy.

That night, neither Lou nor I listened very intently. In fact, he was planning on sneaking out the back door when everybody bowed his head to pray. Suddenly the preacher came out with some kind of prophecy and Lou knew it was right to him. The first time the preacher said it, Lou didn't catch it and said out loud,

> Lord, if that was for me, say it again. I wasn't listening.

So, the Lord said it again!

Suddenly Lou got right up out of his seat and headed for the altar. He knelt and the preacher stopped preaching and laid hands on Lou's head. Other people joined their hands to his. Lou started muttering another language and he received the baptism of the Holy Spirit. It was beautiful, and he got up with a shining face looking like a newborn. He was just that—a newborn, happy and free of his old self.

If that guy can do that I know it's got to be real.

Sister Phillips leaned over and said,

> Leah, you get to the altar and receive the baptism of the Holy Spirit.

She almost pushed me up the aisle. They laid hands on me and I felt a warm rush coming up from my feet to the top of my head. I thought I was going to explode. It was much stronger than drugs could ever be. It was a warm feeling and sort of a cold feeling—like standing in front of an airconditioner and burning up at the same time. I started speaking in tongues. For awhile, I couldn't get words out. I just wanted to say, "Praise the Lord." Suddenly, the words that came weren't mine. Someone was giving me words and it wasn't the preacher. It was my Lord. I was shaking so hard I couldn't stand up. My legs wouldn't hold me and Sister Phillips put a chair under me before I fell. It was a fantastic experience! I mean it was absolutely unbelievable.

I knew then that the Lord was surely at work in my behalf. I couldn't have done it myself. Even with drugs, I couldn't have done it. No drugs I ever took could have done it. The Lord knew I needed an experience that strong because He knew what I needed for me to believe He was real. Now He had given me my own experience and I didn't have to take anybody else's word for it. Somehow, even when I saw the crippled girl walk, it was thrilling, but it still was not happening to me. When I started stammering in tongues, I knew I was completely changed.

Teen Challenge has offered me a chance to go to their home in Garrison, New York. I want to go, but I hate leaving Sister Phillips. She is a radiant, beautiful person and I call her Mom because she is my spiritual mother. Maybe I lean on her too much.

If I leave here I would also be leaving my probation officer so leaving isn't all bad. From the beginning I've been scared of him. He has a terrible reputation for sending kids to prison and is supposed to be a cold-blooded dragnet cop. He was dead set against it when the judge let me go home with Sister Phillips.

I'd rather see you in prison than see you on drugs.

His face was frozen stiff when he said it and I knew I was headed for the pen. I used to go to his office really stoned and nodding all over the place while trying to act straight in front of him. I couldn't do it. He knew I was playing around and wasn't living up to my probation. No wonder he was against me—but it seemed like everybody was against me—the federal people from Lexington and all my counselors on drug programs, my friends and my parents. I got kicked out of two beauty schools and had enrolled in a third but had to quit, because I was so strung out on drugs I couldn't hack it.

If I was sick, I'd have to leave and go get dope. If I was stoned, I couldn't work because I'd be nodding out, scaring half the kids. It was bad. Drugs headed me right toward prison and I was afraid of prison because I had more enemies in prison than out. From some, I had stolen money. From others, I had taken money, told them I was going to bring back dope and never went back. Sometimes, I would steal some of their dope and fill their bags with sugar. I knew if I ran into some of these people in prison I'd get my head beaten in.

To stay longer in Houston would have been stagnation. The Lord was showing me that it's possible to grow only so much before going on to other growing opportunities.

Whether I went to New York or Los Angeles at the end of the three months depended, not only on whether Teen Challenge continued to see me as a good risk, but whether they had room for me in one place or the other.

From the beginning I was afraid of L.A. For me to be in the middle of a city

where the action is

was asking for trouble. I tried to leave it up to the Lord as to which program, but I continued to register my complaints with Him against Los Angeles and gave Him my "druthers."

It was another tense period of waiting. Never in Sister Phillips' home had I broken into cold sweats until it was time to leave. Fear of the unknown made me insecure, but she kept telling me it was normal. From what she said, I knew the Teen Challenge Home in Garrison, New York, was a long way from New York City. It was in the country which seemed to remove more temptations than downtown L.A. The day came when Mrs. Phillips said,

Today your acceptance letter came, Leah.

I didn't know whether to laugh or cry, but something told me by the sound of her voice that I was going to Garrison, my first choice. She hugged me and we spread tears over each other knowing we would part. My folks were called, they helped me arrange transportation, and Mom took me shopping. The distance between us was great although she fully approved of my flying to Garrison and continuing in the Teen Challenge program.

After good-byes were said and the plane roared away from Houston, I shook with excitement and prayed on a leaning-on-the-Lord prayer. It was long and very deep because He was leading me every mile, opening new opportunities for growth.

He was with me all the way.

The Walter Hoving Home is part of Teen Challenge and is run by the director, the Reverend John Benton, and his wife. It is a beautiful three-story Tudor mansion in Garrison, New York. I don't know how many rooms, but to me it looked like it was right out of a movie. Texas is completely flat, hardly a hill. Garrison, New York, looked like heaven.

I can't believe it. An ex-addict like me
living in this beautiful mansion.

The girl laughed. I guess she didn't realize how beautiful everything was.

How long you been on drugs?

Five years.

What drugs have you been on?

I named every known kind because I took anything I could get. She didn't bat an eye and I knew she had heard it all before.

Smiling, she handed me a Teen Challenge rule book.

NO SMOKING, NO ALCOHOL, NO DRUGS,
PROMPTNESS, COOPERATION, DISCIPLINE
AUTOMATIC DISMISSAL

Open your suitcase, Leah.

My suitcase, Mrs. Benton?

Then it slowly dawned on me she was checking for drugs. It triggered my memory of jail when they checked out, not only my belongings, but clothing right down to my bare skin. She lifted out each piece of clothing and tried not to shake it but feel it for pills or paraphernalia. It was her way of saying I trust you, but I don't trust you.

At first, I resented it, but Mrs. Benton was a far cry from a jail matron and I felt she had a right to check my belongings. After all, she and her husband had taken me sight unseen. She knew it was my first trip out of Texas and it was my first day away from under Sister Phillips' wing. She had a right not to trust me. Maybe I couldn't trust myself, yet I knew enough not to smuggle the enemy into the Lord's new plan for my life.

I liked Mrs. Benton from the beginning. She reminded me somewhat of Sister Phillips, but they had never met. Right away I knew she was sympathetic but not permissive. She seemed tenderly interested and concerned about each girl.

Leah, every morning we have breakfast at eight and prayers at nine for half an hour. Everybody prays but not always aloud. Some girls read their Bibles for thirty minutes. Three days a week we have required chapel and Bible classes until noon. We study Old Testament, New Testament, and practical Christian living. We even have a Dale Carnegie course which is fun and I think everything we do brings you seventeen girls closer together. I hope you'll be happy with us.

As days passed I learned a lot about the Bible, but discovered early it was easier to study it than to practice it. Practicing was something else.

Keeping rules was the hardest.

In the second week I was five minutes late for work detail.

> For being late you get an extra hour.

What's an hour?

> It's when you work an extra hour in a job I give you. Saturday and Sunday are the only days you get off and if you have too many extra work hours they are made up on your free days.

What happens now that I'm late?

> Scrub the pipes in the basement.

I couldn't believe Reverend Benton. I thought he must be kidding. Suddenly in a great flash of good sense, I decided to hold my temper and headed for bucket and rag.

The basement was dark, low, and very hot, to match my temper. Stooping down, I sized up the job and took to the big pipes first. Between soot, sweat, and blood pressure my language hit a new peak. No one heard me. I sloshed water everywhere and made several trips to the kitchen for clean water while swearing at the girls who had smart comments about how I looked. At first, I bucked the assignment, then decided to accept it. I tried to find shortcuts to simplify the discipline, trying to tell myself this was part of learning to be a Christian. Then I couldn't see that it had anything at all to do with being a Christian and broke down in tears. Between tears, sweat, and soot the whole experience stands out in my mind as one great afternoon of hate. Most important, however, I didn't quit. First, because I knew it was possible for them to double my time in the basement, and second, because I knew I had to learn to work and keep my cool. That alone was a new experience for me.

I had been used to having people agree with me. If people didn't agree with me, I'd either get stoned or cut off their dope supply.

For awhile at Hoving Home, I couldn't sleep. I was mired in anxiety and tension—worrying over whether I could make it through the Teen Challenge program. After all, the Lexington drug program had tagged me a hopeless drug addict. So had three other programs. I would sleep about an hour and lie awake the rest of the night. I was still on probation, the program was very strict, and I had a terrific fear of going back to jail. The smallest details marched across my brain like they were orders from headquarters.

I would cry and pray and try to sleep, but the harder I prayed the more uptight I got. At one point, I thought I was going to crack up and was ready to beg the counselors to send me back to jail because I couldn't make it. Now I know it was the devil trying to get me discouraged.

Then I became terrified they might feel I was insincere—that I was using them. I'd think, that counselor doesn't like me, or, since I've been in jail, they don't really trust me. I was paranoid over people not liking me. One day it worked itself out in class. We were talking about worrying and the Lord's words,

Be not anxious for tomorrow will be anxious for itself.

I started thinking about it.

But I think it's good to worry. Somebody in the world has to worry.

No, that's not scriptural. Nobody has to worry. The Lord does the worrying for you. It's good to be concerned about people's problems, but it's not good to worry about them. There's a difference between being concerned and being worried.

Yeah, there is. I never thought of it before.

I thought it was my Christian duty to be worried about somebody or I wasn't a true friend. Now I see it's better to be concerned about them, pray for them, and leave the burdens with the Lord. For a long time, I would give them to the Lord and keep taking them back.

Okay, Lord, I'm not going to worry about it.

Then I'd start worrying again. I was taking on the Lord's work. After I got this straightened out in my mind, I wasn't so high-strung.

Thank You, Jesus, for giving me fourteen hours sleep last night. I honestly thought I was going to backslide without it. You are faithful not to allow me to suffer above what I am able. I guess You knew I wasn't able to take much more without flipping out. Forgive me, Lord, for griping and thanks for teaching me things even when I don't want to learn . . . like trusting in You.

Today is my first New Year's Day in Christ. I've been saved almost four months now. Hoving Home is beautiful with its twenty-three acres of land and the cold, clear stream making its way to the Hudson. We had a beautiful Christmas and on several occasions I stood like a newborn before the crèche we made. I am a newborn Christian with much to learn, yet I am old enough to know that He was born for goodness and came to be my example for loyal living. No shepherd could have been more excited on the night of His birth and no angel more jubilant. He lived for me. He died for me and I press on, like St. Paul, to carry every mark of a Christian.

My roommate is only seventeen and she is so sensitive I'm afraid to talk with her—let alone kid around with her. I'm afraid I'll hurt her feelings.

Help me, Lord.

Today I had an argument with the counselor. She didn't like my folk music. I got mad, ran upstairs, and slammed the door.

Later I apologized, even though I don't see what is wrong with it, but, if my type of music is that important to me, it needs to go for that reason alone.

I've been hung up on things before. In fact, I was so hung up I got arrested seven times and went all the way down trying to prove I was somebody who could defend her hang-ups.

The furthest down I got was when I was kicking drugs in an isolation cell. They put me in isolation because I fought all the time.

In isolation I was totally abandoned.

Nobody came near to talk, to ease my cramps, to bring me down easy with Methadone, or offer a helping hand.

I remember I kept feeling like I had to throw up but hadn't eaten anything. My heaving didn't bring anything but sore muscles. No one came to ease the pain. I was nothing but skin and bones laying on a bunk with a horse blanket over me. My legs ached and I was freezing to death. At the same time, I was sweating. Finally, I braced my aching legs up against the cement walls and it eased them while I held my aching head. Every time I felt like I had to throw up, I tried to get over to the dirty little toilet but couldn't make it. Finally, I just threw up all over the blanket. I was so sick I didn't even bother trying to get up anymore and rolled from side to side on the bed aching and heaving.

When the matron came she was furious.

Clean up that mess.

I'm not going to clean it up. I'm sick.

But I cleaned it up. She made me.

It took months for me to realize that, if I had never gone to jail, I would never have stopped running long enough to think whether or not I wanted to change. I was so hung up on getting high and playing my ego game I couldn't take time to think. As long as I was high, I'd forget about all the times I was sick. In fact, I could be sick all day long, but, as soon as I'd get that needle in my arm, I'd forget about it until I was sick again.

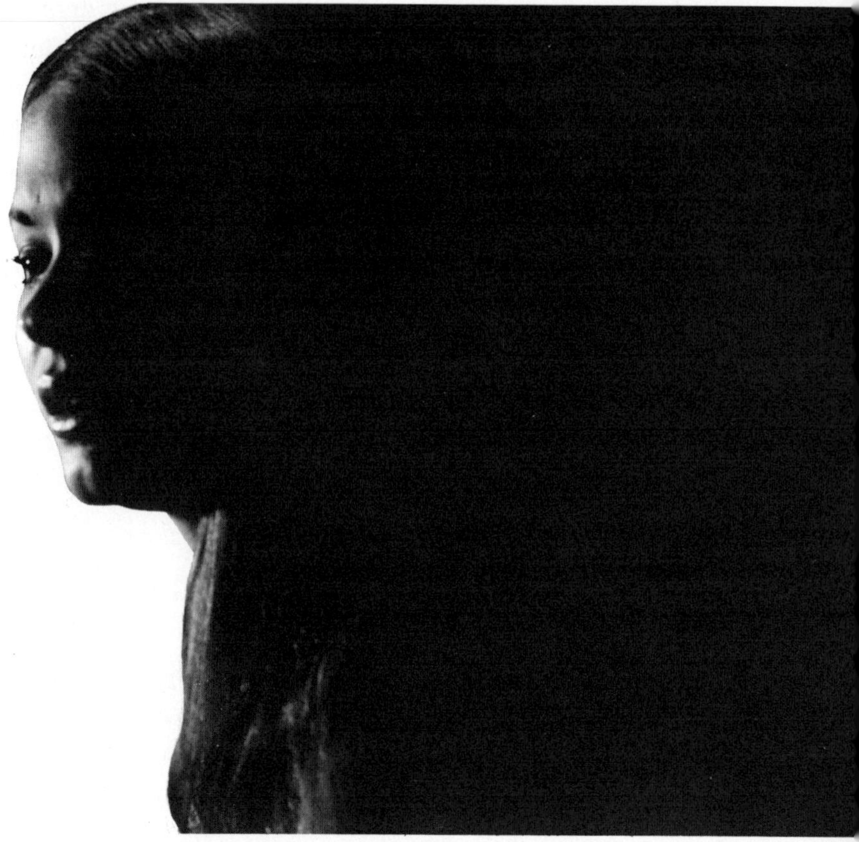

In jail, I couldn't forget about drugs because I was sick the whole time. Earlier when I kicked, I was in a mental hospital where they keep you so doped up you don't really feel much of it. I used to go in the hospital just to get my habit down to where I could support it without too much sweat.

In the isolation cell, I was really down and started to think and couldn't see myself spending the rest of my life in the pen. I had friends who would get arrested once or twice and they would go to the pen for three years or more. Then they would get out. After a third offense on a felony in Texas, they give you life. In the deep recesses of my mind, I could see myself eventually doing life and ending up like every junkie in there—just skin and bones with half my teeth knocked out.

I couldn't hack that.

My old life was full of enemies who hated me. I had either turned them on, turned them on and dropped them, or wouldn't let them stop drugs.

My new life was full of the rules at Hoving Home. They were what I needed and I knew

The Lord had worked it out for me.

Today, I don't see how I could have been on drugs. I didn't know I was unusually bad until I was bad off, and then it seemed like I was proud of my badness. Now, in fact, I believe I was obsessed with being bad and didn't know it until I became a Christian.

Now I can't be that way. I'm the me that I was supposed to be in the first place.

Praise the Lord!

Helen left last month to go to Phoenix House, a secular drug program in New York City, but today she is back as my roommate. She is playing games and I wonder whether the counselors will catch on. I wonder, too, whether she will let me get through that wall she has built around her soul. I like her. She is a good kid only she doesn't realize she is on a dead-end street. She is only seventeen and already somebody stabbed her in the back in Central Park. Can't she see she can't make it her way?

Lord, help me get across to her that You are real and You are what she has been looking for all her life. Make her miserable if that's what it takes for her to see her need—she is just a kid. No one can reach her. Anoint me with Your spirit so I can tell her what she needs to hear.

Today Helen got caught smoking twice and Terry found some Methadone tablets on her. She will be dismissed if she doesn't cool it.

Well, it happened. Helen left. Not only because she was kicked out, but because she wanted sex and drugs more than she wanted to go to heaven. She lied to me and it hurt.

Now I know how my mom felt when I was lying to her. Once she came home while I was fixing heroin. I was in the kitchen; didn't know she was coming home early.

I had just pulled the needle out of my arm and the spoon and everything were laying on the table. Quickly, I grabbed them and threw them behind the refrigerator as she walked in. Right away she was suspicious.

She looked around trying to decide what to say and do.

> What's wrong?

Nothing.

> Let me see your arm.

She whisked across the kitchen grabbing for it. Blood was still dripping where the needle had been and she reached a decision which sent me to another jail cell.

I'm going to call the police.

I didn't think she would but she did. In fact, she drove me to the station and had me charged with possession of narcotic paraphernalia. In Texas that meant two to ten years. But when it came time to go to court, she wouldn't testify against me. Once again, I knew she had hope that I could kick drugs and return to a wholesome life. I look back upon this as one of the greatest expressions of Mom's belief in me. If she had testified against me, I would still be in the pen.

Once, when I got out of jail, she took me to a mental hospital and I was furious. She said it was for people with nervous breakdowns. I didn't want to go, stayed only a month, and went right back on drugs. She took me to five other hospitals—one of them was the state mental hospital. It didn't work either. I ran away with a guy who was also trying to kick his habit.

For awhile, I forged checks on my mother to get money for my habit. Once it reached a total of $2,000, but she didn't find out until the end of the month, and in between I stayed high and out of sight.

I used to steal her blind.

Twice I robbed our house, but she wrote me in a hospital that she had paid off the checks. That was when I ran away from the hospital. I just wanted to get my habit down and get her off my back.

The boy I ran away with was really crazy. He robbed stores and had a lot of legal heat on him. He was an out-and-out gangster. When you're on drugs it seems as if you go to jail every couple of months. Associating with known criminals can revoke one's probation, and I was forever on probation.

At the federal hospital in Lexington they told me I was a hopeless drug addict. This blew my mind because I knew people who had been on drugs twenty or thirty years and were accepted for treatment, but, because I had failed on five other drug treatment programs, they wouldn't take me.

I was a hopeless case, a bad risk.

Now I can see the Lord's hand in this. If I had gone to the hospital, I doubt that I would have become a Christian. I might have, but I doubt it.

My folks spent thousands of dollars sending me to psychiatrists, medical doctors, hospitals, and cures. They thought I had a mental problem and all the time it was a spiritual one. I wasn't from the ghetto which most people associate with drug addicts. I had had everything and for a long time Mom couldn't believe I was on drugs. She thought I was kidding. As she woke up to the facts, she used to cry all the time and worry herself sick over me.

She couldn't believe that either I or my sis was on drugs and would express her fear of them, or quote something she heard about how many kids were hooked.

Once, when my sis was taking a bath, Mom found a reefer in the pocket of some blue jeans. She thought we had put it there just to scare her or make a joke. By then we were full-fledged pot smokers.

During my commitments to hospitals and jails, when she visited me, she looked unnatural. I never got used to seeing her through bars, but, as deep as her hurt went, her hope for me went as high.

She would bribe me with a car or something else if I could just stay clean for awhile. My promises meant nothing and she knew it.

We both knew that.

Going home after a jail or hospital term was only a temporary arrangement. It was a matter of time before I would run away or be in more trouble.

Once after I was a Christian, Mrs. Phillips went home with me and it was as difficult for her as for me. My folks belong to a church, but they weren't evangelistic in the least. The strain of visiting and making trite conversation became so difficult, Mrs. Phillips and I left.

Today Mom and I get along fine. My folks are behind me 100 percent and Mom is helping the Ladies' Auxiliary for Teen Challenge.

As I write, my mind is on Helen. Suzie told me to shake the dust off my feet about Helen and forget I ever knew her. Why, Jesus, does Helen turn her back on the truth and make such weak decisions? I tried my best to win her for You. Maybe I scared her away. Did I try too hard to get her saved on my own power instead of Yours? Will I see her in heaven?

> Many things about tomorrow
> I don't seem to understand,
> But I know who holds tomorrow
> And I know who holds my hand.

Copyright © 1950 by Singspiration, Inc. All rights reserved. Used by permission.

Lord send me a Spanish roommate who really wants to make it—one who is desperate and is willing to accept You, Jesus.

Well, my new roommate came today. She is a pretty Italian junkie named Kathy. Suzie, down the hall, wanted an Italian roommate and I a Spanish one, so the Lord compromised and I got an Italian who looks Spanish.

*She is interested, Jesus,
but I don't want to push You at her.*

I might blow her mind. We stayed up late rapping. She has been through a lot, but her folks enrolled her and she has no personal will to stay.

I've just finished reading Job, Lord. You've wanted me to read him for a long time and I thought he didn't relate to me. I thought the story was about a grouchy old man who sat around feeling sorry for himself. But Job was righteous and he had reasons to complain, but he was wrong for questioning Your existence. This is what I've been doing with my superiors here . . .

questioning.

I have complaints against the rules and complaints against the people. My complaints seem legitimate, but I'm still wrong. Forgive me, Lord, and help me grow stable instead of drifting back and forth. Job kept hoping You cared about him personally and his friends told him to believe blindly. They were wrong for judging and Job was wrong for questioning and hoping.

Kathy left today. She couldn't make it. The rules were too stiff and she was too weak. *Keep Your eyes on her and save her soul in Your own time and way, Lord.*

With drugs the mental habit is a lot harder to kick than the physical. If Kathy, like other girls here, could just get her mind off drugs and turned on to Jesus, she wouldn't be satisfied with drugs. I remember for a long time I couldn't keep my mind off drugs rationalizing that, even if I went back on drugs at least my habit wouldn't be so big. Then I'd think: You've come this far, Leah. It's stupid to go back.

Today here at Hoving Home I was looking through my scrapbook and found this poem that I wrote in an isolation cell at the county jail.

Freedom

Hope has faded
Bitterness reigns,
The mind weary
The soul chained.

I can't help wondering how I went on without knowing You, Lord. I was so low. I knew my soul was hungry and that I was at the bottom of my rope in total emptiness. How much time I wasted! I kept looking for one thing, then another. Help me make the right decisions from here on, Lord. I can't afford another mistake.

When I think of total emptiness I think about my car wreck in 1967.

I was on LSD that night.

Two of us were on it, but the driver was clean. He kept watching us acting silly. As we were crossing a busy intersection under the freeway, he ran a red light and got hit broadside by two cars. It happened so fast I didn't even duck. Glass flew everywhere and I thought, Wow, this is it. This is how I'm going to die and you only die once so I've got to sit up and watch. This is the ultimate trip. It was weird. I don't know how my thoughts got that way. I didn't want to die. Never in all my drug trips did I want to kill myself, but never did I want to live either.

When the car stopped spinning, I couldn't figure out whether I was dead or alive. I thought, Wow, if I'm dead, then death is the same thing as life, but, if I'm alive, I've got to start answering the questions that cop keeps asking.

What color was the light?

What color was the light?

I repeated,

What color was the light?

I started to laugh. I laughed so hard he thought I was hysterical. Maybe I was.

The car was totalled and it wasn't long before my stomach started swelling from internal bleeding. I could hardly stand up. After an ambulance trip, and a week in the hospital, they discovered I had a ruptured kidney and two broken ribs.

Day and night, kids came to visit me in the hospital. They would go into the bathroom and shoot themselves with speed. Right away I started doing it, too.

Once Mom came in my hospital room and I wanted her to think I was in hysterics, but I was really, really stoned. My eyes were twice their size, but she didn't know what to look for to identify drugs. I hadn't slept for three days and she thought that was my problem. My eyes scared me when I looked in the mirror, but she didn't notice anything very different.

It must be great to die.

> You'll feel better in the morning.

I think she was afraid to say,

> Don't say that, don't say that.

It might blow my mind and I would go into shock. That day, I don't think she ever knew I was on acid. She does now. I admitted it to her later on. Sometimes I felt that I was hurting her on purpose, trying to get back at her for the past.

My sister came to the hospital that same day and immediately said,

Wow, you're stoned!

She didn't stay.

The night of the accident was the last time I ever took acid. Up to then it would send me on a giggly, happy trip. After the accident, acid made me sad. The whole world situation overwhelmed me with people starving and dying. I was obsessed with the aching loneliness of mankind and, since there was nothing I could do about it, I would cry. Everything anybody said hurt me deeply and I wasn't sobbing-crying, but tears would pour out of my eyes. For awhile I thought I was losing my mind and it scared me.

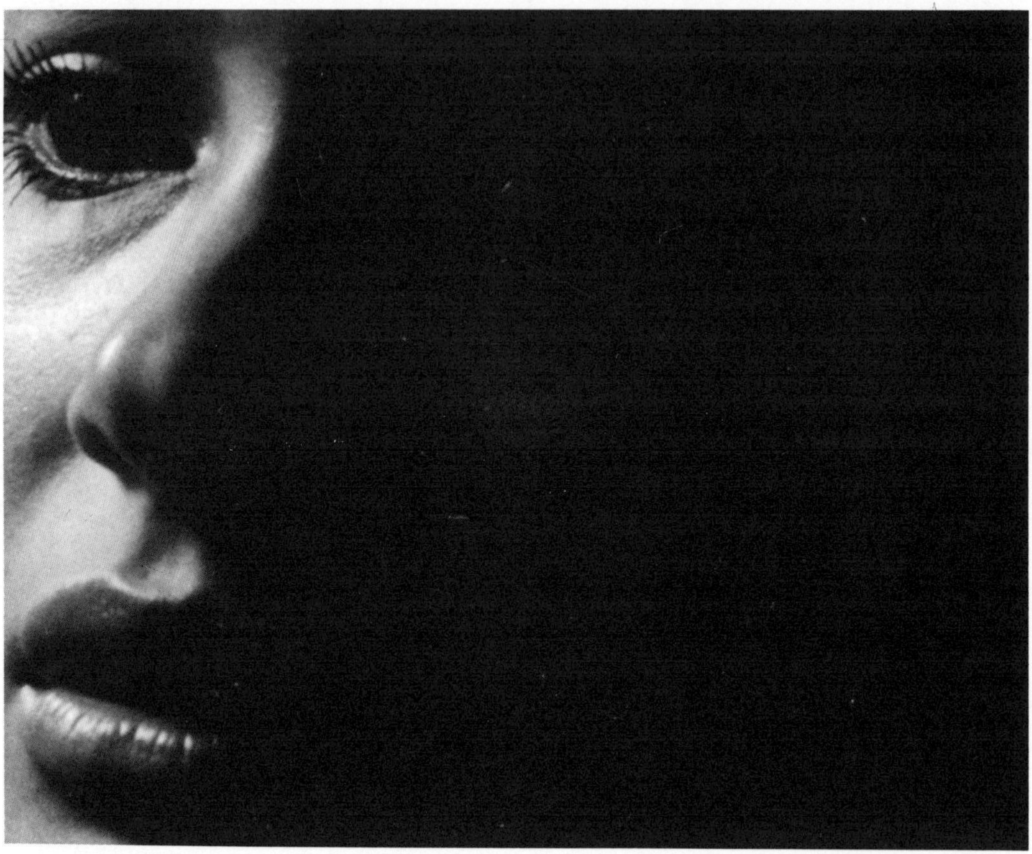

When I went on speed I liked it for awhile, but it made me self-conscious. The only thing I liked about it was the first rush. After that it got to be monotonous and made me think things like, These people aren't really my friends. Speed made me paranoid so I graduated to heroin with Randy's help. With heroin I forgot about everything. Nothing mattered.

Lord, I never knew the world was bright until I met You. I used to not be able to see past my own dingy little world and now each bird in the colorful autumn trees chirps out,

Jesus loves you.

Do You want me to go back with Randy, Jesus? He writes from prison that he believes in You. He even quit smoking and goes to Bible classes. He's been in almost two years now. Maybe he is hoping religion will help him make parole. Maybe not.

How well I remember the night he overdosed on me. I was on the telephone.

Look, I've got to hang up. I've got two guys here
and they are both overdosing.

Frantically I dived for Randy. He wasn't even breathing. I screamed, hoping Pete would rally and help, but he was out cold. I slapped, rubbed, and shook Randy, but nothing brought him out of it. He was heavy and I pulled him toward a chair, propped him up, and with all my might got him on his feet. I knew if he slumped down he was a goner. I kept yelling at him to stand up and try to walk. All the time I kept watching Pete immovable on the floor. Randy stood swaying and I braced him against me. We walked a few steps and he started to fall. I grabbed his jacket and it tore up the side, but he muttered something. I kept yelling at him to walk and, when he did, I jumped toward Pete, trying the same solution. It worked, but just in time.

Several times I overdosed.

I had taken some barbiturates that morning and heroin at noon. The combination is bad. I had just fixed, turned around and said,

Hey, I feel bumblebee stings all over me.

I tried to stay on my feet but pitched headlong into a bookcase. The corner of it hit me in the right eye. It's a wonder I didn't knock my eye out. My friend Bruce ran for help from the Vietnam medic living two doors away.

They said I was turning blue and had no pulse until the medic gave me heart massage. I kept up a steady rattle in my throat and they called the ambulance. I started to gasp and choke before the ambulance arrived, but they took me anyway.

In the emergency room I had one of the greatest scares of my life when I saw a policeman. I thought I had been arrested again. As it turned out, he was always on duty there. The hospital was obligated to call my mom and I remember my mom screaming,

> Where did you get those needle marks?

Why didn't you let me die, man?

My memory remains alive with details of experiences from drugs, but none is more real or regretted than when a friend died from drugs I had sold him. He was twenty years old and wanted to get into our crowd. Getting in meant going along with the games we played.

You're not used to taking anything this heavy.

> I can handle it. No problem.

But this is good stuff and I'm even overdosing on it, man. I know it's too strong for you.

It was my only warning to him.

It didn't take long before I saw he was on a bad trip. He fell to the floor and was out cold. We gave him the salt water treatment, but it didn't work.

He died.

All of us in the room were filled with a mixture of panic and regret.

>What happens now?
>>Would we be jailed?
>>>Would we be blamed?
>
>Yes, to all that.

After awhile I brushed off the incident with,

Well, I warned him!

What I learned later was that he had had a heart condition for several years and heart trouble doesn't mix with drugs. Funny, he hadn't mentioned it, but then maybe he felt he was going to die soon and wanted to have a wing-ding before wrapping it all up.

> Maybe he wanted to belong.
> Maybe he gambled his heart against his kicks.
> I don't know.

I only know that I have grieved over my sin in turning him on, and pray regularly for his family. My feeble warning to him was not really a warning at all. I wanted to turn him on. After all, I was his supplier and he was another customer. I wanted his money.

When I am alone here at Hoving Home I think and remember the bad days in my other life, praying for a solution in building a better life.

Sometimes I get lonely here, Lord. Please, Lord, send along the right guy if Randy's not the one. Then prepare his heart for it so my new relationship won't damage his relationship with You.

Now that I'm on the right track, Jesus, I have to make up for all the years wasted. I know You want me to spread Your gospel so I need to go to school. I can't teach more about You than I know myself. What Bible school do you want me to go to? Show me a sign so I'll know for sure.

Today is my birthday. I've been alive twenty-one years, but this is my first spiritual birthday. For twenty-one years I've been walking around dead and now I've been born again.

A couple of years ago I thought I was alive when I was hustling in the streets. After all, robbery and forgery didn't net me enough and after Randy got sent to prison how else could I support my $150-$250 a day heroin habit? I was dependent on him.

I was doing three and a half to four papers of heroin a day. A paper is a gram of heroin and a gram costs $45 in Texas.

A half-gram costs $23.

For awhile, I thought I could stay stoned on half a gram a day, but after awhile a half-gram would barely take the sick off.

Who wants to spend $23 just to be normal?

So I'd take pills, too, until I could manage to get something better. I could tell when I had to have something stronger, because my eyes would begin to water and I'd have hot and cold flashes. Then my nose would run and I'd get pains in my legs and back.

Once Mom threw me out of the house because she had had it. We had a big thing about her expecting me to be something I didn't want to be. I left without bag and baggage and spent the next few weeks sponging off everybody I knew until I got myself together.

Then one day I met a girl who told me she could show me a way to support my habit without any sweat, and all the proceeds were pure gravy.

She was a prostitute.

We talked about it for a little while, but it didn't take me long to decide to give it a trial run.

What did I have to lose?

After all I had tried everything else and was sick half the time wanting dope and couldn't pay for it.

> It's easy. Stand in bars and watch for guys. After a few days in a bar they'll spot you and the rest is simple.

I don't know if I could get a guy to go for me.

>Honey, some go for anything in skirts. You'll see.

What about pregnancy?

>No trouble if you're on heroin. It's a natural contraceptive.

Then there's no danger of pregnancy. I'm on it so bad I can hardly support my habit.

>You'll be able to support it now.

 I believed her and picked a bar where I thought a high-class type of male would be. After the first couple of days, I could see how easy it was and changed bars to keep from getting involved steadily with the same guys. Involvement wouldn't leave me time to spend my cash on stuff and enjoy a high.

 It kept me busy picking bars, keeping appointments, and bar-hopping. Constantly, I tried to think of shortcuts to get the money and cut out on a guy.

One day I discovered that the girl who taught me worked a book. She carried it everywhere and as weeks went by she stopped hitting the bars in favor of calling her men for appointments. Her listings were business and professional men in Houston. Some paid enough to support her habit for a whole day, depending on how long she stayed with them. When I suggested that she split her list with me, she got mad.

From the beginning, I was supposed to give her 40 percent of everything I made, but she knew I was cheating on her. I learned to beat her at her own game and was getting more business and cheating more than she ever dreamed.

One day I got fed up and called a friend saying,

I can't stand this girl anymore. She's driving me
crazy and is expecting too much of a cut.

Together we devised a way to copy her entire book of 200-300 names, but it took her less than a week to discover that I was meeting in hotels and bars the doctors, lawyers, and Indian chiefs from her book. She was furious and we became bitter enemies. Enemy? I had more than I could count and adding her didn't panic me.

The prostitution game was just another game and I was winning. To make it even better I learned that in Texas an arrested hustler gets only ninety days if caught while robbery and forgery get you five to ten.

I stuck to prostitution.

Money came easier than it had since Randy got jailed and life took on a rosy future that lasted about ten days.

I moved in with two guys who allowed me to stay rent-free if I helped support their drug habits. One guy had been a burglar, but he stopped working when he found out how much I was making. They were using me so I split.

Where could I go? I couldn't go home and my probation officer had a warrant out for my arrest. Besides that I was broke.

To help meet my dilemma I called a name out of my book,

> got paid $40 by some cheapskate,
> stole $40 more off him,
> and got stoned.

Later I decided to straighten up and report to the probation officer, thinking he would let me off again. When I walked into his office, he didn't even speak but got up out of his chair and put handcuffs on me, walked me across the street to jail where I stayed four months.

For the first time, it dawned on me that I wasn't on top of the game anymore. Before this I had been able to beat everyone out of anything. I had been mooching, scheming, and best of all, winning. Now everybody was playing me and I was losing. The walls were closing in and I was stuck in a rut.

Now I'm out of the rut for good, Jesus, waiting for a sign about school. I'm ready to go where You want me to go, but first could You send me a roommate who doesn't snore?

She committed suicide, Lord. She was thirty-one with a little seven-year-old daughter. She taught me to hustle and here I am crying and praying for her.

> You should get straight and you should quit shooting dope. You'll wind up like me if you keep going.

Who are you to tell me?

Then she wouldn't say anything more.

Now she's dead.

Overdosed on purpose because they were going to charge her with being an habitual criminal! It hurts me.

Some of the girls graduate from the program soon. They don't want to leave and I guess I won't either when it's my turn. Hoving Home grows on us. There is always fear of what is ahead, but You, Jesus, control my unknowns so I don't worry about the future.

Hallelujah!

The signs are coming. Two graduates are going to a Bible College in North Dakota. Neither girl has flown in a plane and they are excited. (One girl from New York City had never seen a cow before she came here.)

Yesterday I got my first sign from You, Lord, about school. I saw a big ad about Central Bible College in Springfield, Missouri. It sounded great. Do You really suppose they would take me? Will the kids accept me? I'm leaving it up to You, remember. If You want me to go there keep showing me signs.

Many things about tomorrow
I don't seem to understand,
But I know who holds tomorrow
And I know who holds my hand.

Copyright © 1950 by Singspiration, Inc.
All rights reserved. Used by permission.

Yes I do, Lord, yes I do.

My roommate still snores, Lord. Are you trying to teach me patience? I prayed that I wouldn't get a roommate who was emotional, but she's got problems. I wish I could help her care about her looks. Today I cut her scraggly hair, fixed it, and told her she would be pretty if she would lose weight. She thinks she is hopeless. Last night she woke up screaming Your name. I prayed with her, but I don't know if she is ready for You yet.

Today is Halloween—a pagan holiday. But it's also a day the Lord has made so I shall rejoice and be glad in it.

The girls here at Hoving Home aren't weeded out by anyone but themselves. Some of them can't take the rules while others can't get their minds off drugs.

73

Sometimes we don't get along, like last night at dinner when we were talking about someone in the news who had been stabbed.

I told them about a guy I knew. Mandy gave me a dirty look and told me to stop talking at the dinner table about stabbing. She said, not only did it make her mad, it made her sick.

What's the matter? Sometimes I get the feeling
nobody wants to talk to me. Do you want me to
leave? I'll leave if you want me to. Sometimes I
get the feeling I can't even relate to you people—
like I'm on some kind of a different wavelength
giving everybody bad vibes or something.

With that I got up and left the table. Later I apologized to Mandy because I realized it was Laura I was mad at, and I had taken it out on Mandy.

Laura came up later.

>You know you said at dinner that maybe you were
>giving people bad vibes or something?

Yeah?

Well, you are. Sometimes I get the feeling you're so critical of people you think nobody is good enough to be around you.

I don't think I complain that much, and when I complain it's legit. I'm not just making up a big lie. I've been trying hard not to complain, but it seems like the more I try the more people accuse me of it.

You have a negative attitude about some people.

Have I?

I started thinking: Yeah, in a way I guess I have. It hurt me when Laura said it, but I knew it needed to be said and the Lord used her to say it. I talked to her for a long time.

I'm glad you came to me. I really have been trying to do better, but it seems like I can't get it out of me. Do me a favor—when you hear me being critical of others, just tell me about it.

To some people, just saying the weather is lousy can really be a complaint, and to other people it's a statement. This is one of my worst problems—looking at things from the bad side. That's why I like Laura so much. She told me what I needed to hear while others would agree with me and be friendly. But what good are they if they aren't helping me grow spiritually? If I needed something said, it might hurt for awhile, but in the long run it would be better. The whole experience brought Laura and me closer together.

Wanda helped me, too. She was a girl from Illinois who hadn't been on anything but grass. Her problems were mainly emotional. She was weird, but I liked her.

From the day of her arrival Wanda and I were in competition. We both sang solos in the choir and were both A students. We got along well yet each was jealous of the other. We could sit down and talk through our differences and that was the strength of our relationship. When Wanda was mad at me, she was big enough to tell me why. I would do the same with her. She didn't agree with me very often and told me where I was blind to my own problems. Each of us had a critical spirit when we first came into Teen Challenge, and that same critical nature brought us closer together instead of separating us. We were never best friends, but were something more important—sisters in Christ. We both loved the Lord and wanted others to love Him, too.

Now that both of us are leaving Hoving Home, we will write back and forth hoping to see each other again someday.

Cindy got dismissed today. She wanted to be. Go with her, Lord. Except for Cindy leaving, it's a beautiful day. The girls here are more like my family than my own family. Nobody puts on a phoney front and we want to help each other succeed. After all, Lord, that's what it's all about.

Yesterday Laura and I sang a duet in a Baptist church we visited where we gave testimonies. A man told me I had a Baez quality in my voice.

Praise God!

I couldn't even carry a tune before I got saved.

It won't be long now 'til I leave Hoving Home—it has grown to be my home—to face what, Lord? Only You know.

Today was shadowed when Jennie died of a heart attack. She is better off now. Tell her hello for me, Jesus, and that I'll be praying for her family. She will have a funeral in Harlem but her Hallelujah time is there with You. I'm going to miss my black mom.

Jennie was on stuff for twenty years and lived the last two as a clean Christian. She had come a long way in her thinking and I wonder sometimes why people like this aren't rewarded while they are on earth.

I saw a girl healed who had only a broken wrist, and for awhile I was bitter because Jennie's heart wasn't healed. It seemed like an injustice. Then I realized Jennie's heart WAS healed. I see it now. You healed her heart two years ago and rewarded her by taking her to be nearer You. She didn't have heart trouble—not real heart trouble. Jennie hasn't had heart trouble for two years. I see it now, for the first time.

As to the bones in the wrist—I saw it happen. She came to our meeting and we prayed for her the night before. When she woke up the next morning, she came to me.

> Look!

> It was broken yesterday. It's a miracle.

Like people of old, I might not have believed had I not seen it with my own eyes.

In the past month Bill was healed of an enlarged spleen. After hospital tests, doctors told him he would have to have an operation. He prayed and while the doctors were still standing there he said to them,

> No, I won't have to have an operation. The Lord healed me, Hallelujah!

He got up off the table, walked down the hall, went into the X-ray room, and the spleen was normal.

> We can't understand this!

They thought he was nuts and even thought they had read the original X-rays incorrectly, but Bill knew what had happened and he gave the Lord all the credit.

I know about miracles, Lord, because since You saved me I've never had any desire to do drugs again. I am cured. What could be a greater experience than You?

All the time I was on drugs I realized I was looking for some special experience—the supernatural.

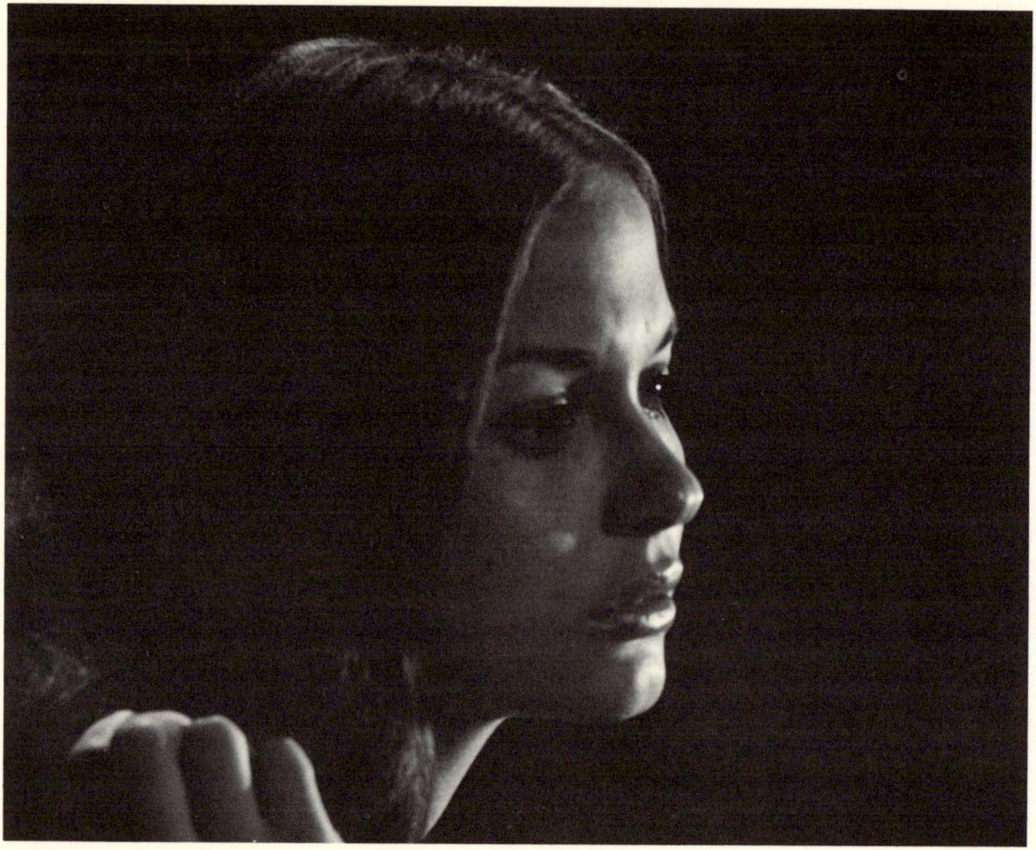

What could be greater than the Lord? Now drugs have nothing to offer me. Ever since I discovered Jesus, I feel sorry for street people without Him. They don't know what they are missing and half of them will never realize it until it's too late.

I'm not empty anymore.

I have Jesus and feel sorry for everybody who doesn't. If they don't have Jesus, they don't have anything at all. It's a pitiful shame.

At Thanksgiving I went home to Houston. After two years away, it gave me a queer feeling. My family had tried to help me, but I never wanted it. They have written me and I sometimes answered, but it was hard to describe to them what had happened to me. I hadn't been homesick and when I saw the house again, I wasn't nostalgic. They were relieved to think I'd made it this far without landing in jail, but I get the feeling they think I'm on a new kind of high and it, too, will pass.

Mom had taken my bedroom furniture to the Teen Challenge halfway house because they needed the space. My sis was married and they had moved into my room. Other clothes were hanging in my closet. I walked from room to room and everything tangible seemed in its place, but I was overwhelmed with intangibles.

There was a feeling that no one was communicating.

After all, how does one start a conversation after two years?

My sis was high on something and so was her husband. So whatever reaching she had done in the two-year span had not been satisfying.

My brother, who to me used to be Mr. All-American Guy, had hair to his shoulders and I hardly knew him.

Mom and my stepdad continued to hide their drinking from me, and when he would hand her a drink, Dad would say,

> Here's your Coke, honey.

I didn't mind that they drank—only that they were trying to put on an act in front of me.

It's hard to put on an act with people you live with. I wanted to say,

It's okay, Dad. I'm older now and have been to hell and back. You don't need to pretend in front of me.

More than that I wanted to say thank you for seeing me through years of tears and experiences that most families never know about except by hearsay. Not many moms know what it means to commit a kid to one mental hospital after another or see her hauled off to jail time after time. Most moms have a general idea what their kids are doing, but I lived two lives—and my second one was so secret I often got caught in lies of my own making and schemes of my own conniving.

I don't blame my folks for not being able to communicate with me. I wouldn't let them. Instead, it was easier to cut out, and that's what I did.

I walked out on them.

From sixth grade on I was walking out on them, trying to play my ego game.

I keep praying that my Houston family will begin to understand my Jesus experience, but don't let me get discouraged on it, Lord. You're never too late. And don't let me get overanxious for the saving of their souls. You'll crack their little games someday, and they'll know peace as they've never know before.

My brother-in-law keeps saying that people are using me. I hope so, Lord.

That's why I was saved.

I want to be a bright light for You and be used by anybody who needs me.

I remember when I put on a rough, hard image to convince everybody I was cool. If I come back now and preach at them, they'll turn me off.

My Houston relationships are turning a corner—not being chopped off. I'll pray for my old friends, but I know Your spirit has to prepare them before they will listen. Just don't let them die and go to hell, Lord.

Today I keep thinking about my application for school. I can't wait to hear from them. It will take more than college acceptance. It will take the acceptance of the kids.

Leaving Hoving Home will be hard, as this has been a cocoon for me to grow wings. At first I was afraid to come, now I'm afraid to go. Over the past two years the easiest thing for me to accept has been

Jesus in my life.

The hardest has been cutting all former ties—completely shutting the book on my old life. Becoming a Christian meant saying,

I don't want ever again to see any of my old friends.
I don't want to go back to them. I don't want to
hang around with them.

They were all I had, but I had to cut them loose—to burn the bridges and start life again

>	without turning back,
>		without calling them,
>			without constantly writing them.

I could look back because it's always good to know where you came from, but I couldn't go back and try to live a Christian life around them. It would be impossible.

Graduation night!

I thought it would never come. I can see why some of the other girls didn't want to leave. I don't want to either, but then again I want to go on to better things for my Lord. Tomorrow opens up new horizons for me. What horizons, I do not know. Every day is a new experience and I can hardly keep up with all the openings the Lord has made for me.

People keep asking what I want to do after college. I'll leave that decision for awhile. Inside I have a vision for a girls' home. It seems as though the Lord is impressing something of that kind of work in my heart. Counseling is my favorite field. I feel my greatest ministry is there. I have a great burden for hippie kids and it seems I don't have as much a burden for junkies or ex-addicts. Kids who are fourteen or fifteen might listen to me.

They are at a crucial age where they can accept the Lord or go down the drain. I'd like to go into coffeehouse work or manage a halfway house. Teen Challenge doesn't take kids under seventeen and I've seen fourteen- and fifteen-year olds in bad shape by that time. Some are already on LSD, thrown out of school, and have nowhere to go for a drug program.

Some of their parents are trying to cover up the problem.
Some have no place to live.
Some have babies.

If they really mean business about dumping drugs, they will make arrangements for their babies somewhere and enter a Teen Challenge program as soon as it is allowed. If they really want to help themselves, they will gladly come on Teen Challenge terms—tough discipline and strict requirements.

Some of them can't give up smoking.
Some can't leave the bottle.
Some can't get off the streets.
Some can't give up partying.

They wouldn't make it in any program because they aren't far down enough. They haven't hit the skids.

Most kids drop programs in the first two months. If they enter a program just because their parents push them, chances are they'll never make it. Some parents are smart enough to see the problem, but can't make the kids realize that it takes personal commitment. Parents cannot do it for their kids. No program is a cure-all. Teen Challenge in New York has a nine-out-of-ten cure rate with girls. It's a fantastic rate.

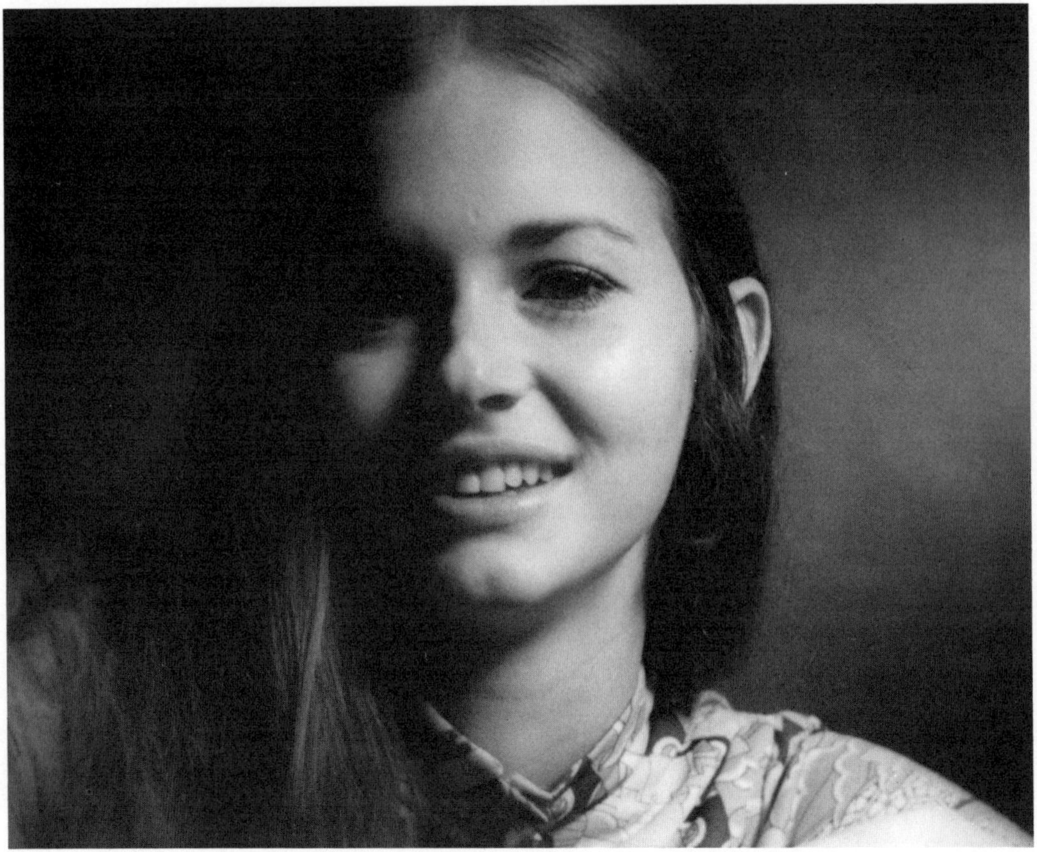

I remember my cell mate saying,

> You've come a long way baby—like down.

Now it's different, Lord.

I wish I could see her and say,

I've come a long way baby—like up!

No more jails, mental hospitals, or street-walking for me. I am sorry I had to come the long route, but I've learned a lot on which to build. Graduation is here and, when I walk that aisle tonight, I don't plan to forget about cleaning the basement pipes, or how it felt to have Mrs. Benton frisk my suitcase for drugs.

College lies ahead and it will be hard.

> I am afraid to leave the cocoon.
> I'm afraid to be with "straight" kids.
> I'm afraid to try my new wings out in the world.

I've fought the fight and finished a part of the course, Lord.

Now help me keep the faith.

I don't know about tomorrow
It may bring poverty,
But the One who feeds the sparrow
Is the One who stands by me,
And the path that be my portion
May be through the flame or flood,
But His presence goes before me,
And I'm covered with His blood.
Many things about tomorrow
I don't seem to understand
But I know who holds tomorrow
And I know who holds my hand.

Copyright © 1950 by Singspiration, Inc.
All rights reserved. Used by permission.

My friend, Bill, used to sing that song in jail after he got saved. You know, Lord, how much I am leaning on it now.